Why Isn't This Marriage Enough?

Why Isn't This Marriage Enough?

How to Make Your Marriage Work
and Love the Life You Have

Sharon Pope

NEW YORK

NASHVILLE • MELBOURNE • VANCOUVER

Why Isn't This Marriage Enough?

How to Make Your Marriage Work and Love the Life You Have

Published in New York, New York, by Morgan James Publishing in partnership with Difference Press. Morgan James is a trademark of Morgan James, LLC.
www.MorganJamesPublishing.com

The Morgan James Speakers Group can bring authors to your live event. For more information or to book an event visit The Morgan James Speakers Group at www.TheMorganJamesSpeakersGroup.com.

Published in New York, New York, by Morgan James Publishing in partnership with Difference Press

ISBN 9781683504085 paperback
ISBN 9781683504092 eBook
Library of Congress Control Number:
2017900432

Cover Design by:
Chris Treccani
www.3dogdesign.net

Interior Design by:
Chris Treccani
www.3dogdesign.net

In an effort to support local communities, raise awareness and funds, Morgan James Publishing donates a percentage of all book sales for the life of each book to Habitat for Humanity Peninsula and Greater Williamsburg.

Get involved today! Visit
www.MorganJamesBuilds.com

Dedication

For Derrick.

You were more than I ever thought possible.

All my love for all my life.

Table of Contents

Section One:

How Did You Get Here?

Chapter 1:

The Truth about Why You Married Him

"Once the realization is accepted that even between the closest human beings infinite distances continue, a wonderful living side by side can grow, if they succeed in loving the distance between them which makes it possible for each to see the other whole against the sky."

RAINER MARIA RILKE

Lynne was 24 years old when she met James. She had recently graduated college and was getting a masters in teaching at the time. She had just gotten out of an intimate and connected relationship that broke her heart in ways she didn't know was possible at such a young age.

James was six years older than Lynne and was nearing the end of his residency to become a pediatrician. He was kind and caring. He was solid and safe. He was smart, responsible and had a brilliant future ahead of him. He checked all the boxes of what she thought she was supposed to have in a partner and she easily saw how they could build a beautiful life together.

Lynne was 27 years old when they married and they had children right away. They had two boys, who are now nine and eleven years old, plus a *whoops* baby girl, who is now six years old. As expected, James is a wonderful father.

They live in a beautiful suburban home, James has a successful practice doing what he loves, and Lynne is smart and beautiful – although she doesn't see herself as others do. Lynne drives a Mercedes minivan, they rent a beach house every year and vacation in South Carolina, her kids go to a great school, and they're thriving in all their after-school activities and sports. James would give her whatever she needs, and if she could tell him what to do to make her feel more loved, more alive and more worthy, he would do it.

James loves his wife.

Lynne's marriage and life appear to be enviable by virtually anyone's standards, so why isn't she happy? Why is this man who loves her, this father who adores his children, this marriage that has lasted thirteen years somehow not enough? She *should* be happy. There is no reason in the world why any reasonable person wouldn't be happy with the life she has.

Lynne, however is struggling to keep her head above water, feeling like she's holding onto an anchor while she tries to continue swimming. As a strong woman, she feels like she needs to be the super-mom, leading many different initiatives: the PTA, the annual holiday play, and the spring carnival. She's running fast and admits that "I can't seem to say no to anyone but my husband." By the time she lays her head down on her pillow at night, she has nothing left to give to either herself or her marriage. She feels empty, lost, and alone.

Lynne has to drink a few glasses of wine in order to have sex with her husband and she hasn't had an orgasm with him in more than five years. Sex is something that she feels she has to do now, rather than something she wants or desires to do. And although she knows she shouldn't feel this way, her husband just seems like one more person needing something from her when she's got nothing left to give.

She feels guilty that she isn't like all the women she sees on Facebook who are perpetually smiling and grateful for their lives – especially because she knows many of them don't have it as good as she does. She made the decisions she made for good, smart, responsible reasons, so why doesn't she feel the way she thought she would? She wonders if she is doing something wrong.

What We Want and Need Changes

What Lynne wanted at age 24 is very different than what Lynne wants now at 40. As a young woman, she was drawn to all the strong qualities James embodied, and it helped that he was older and, in her eyes, more mature. He was perfect marriage material. He wouldn't break her heart as her first love had done.

And he loved her.

At 24, she didn't really know about intimacy and connection. She didn't know about vulnerability and passion. She didn't have to at that time in her life.

There was no lesson plan she missed or handbook she never picked up. She just didn't know what she didn't know. And she didn't know that there's a big difference between what we need and what we want.

Marrying for Safety

When love ends, hearts break. And that heartbreak leaves scars that sometimes we don't heal. Those scars then show up in our fearful thoughts and guide our actions and choices.

We marry the one who won't break our heart.

We stay with the one who everyone else thinks is a great guy.

We choose stability over passion because we don't actually believe we can have both.

Then we end up in a mediocre marriage that we think should be good enough.

He doesn't lie or cheat.

He doesn't hit.

He doesn't hurt. We barely even argue.

Which gives us no good reason to end a relationship. No one will understand and everyone will judge.

My client Bethany needed some safety after her first marriage. She had two children with a man who emotionally and physically abused her for nine years. He drank too much and loved far too little. She feared for herself and the safety of her children and finally left.

So when she met Alex, she was going to choose differently, more wisely than she had before. Alex was lighthearted and fun. Although he didn't have much of a career, he was a leader in their church and he loved being with her children and that was what mattered to Bethany. She needed a good father for her kids much more than she needed an idyllic love affair.

It's so easy to see how we get here. Here, to this place of safety. Here, to this place of stability. Here to this place of having more than we need, but far less than what we want or desire or long for.

It can be harder to see *why* being here doesn't feel good. That's what we are going to explore in the next few chapters: why the life you so carefully cultivated doesn't fulfill you in the ways you imagined it would, and what you can do to change it.

Chapter 2:

The Truth about Your Role

"The difficulty we have in accepting responsibility for our behaviors lies in the desire to avoid the pain of the consequences of that behavior."

M. SCOTT PECK

I had everything I was supposed to have. I did everything I was supposed to do. But something wasn't right and, at some level, I knew that.

I met my first husband in graduate school and we married at 27 years old, after being together for three years. He was (and still is) a good, kind man.

We lived in a four-bedroom home in a suburban golf community. We had nice cars. We took vacations. He worked for the state in IT and I was in marketing in the financial services sector. We had investments, 401Ks, and pension plans. We had one dog and no children.

From the outside looking in, I had no reason to be unhappy; but I was. I was unhappy, lonely, and disconnected.

Most of that is mine to own.

I married my husband because I knew he wouldn't lie to me, cheat on me, or hurt me, as some others had done, and so I became determined to make that relationship last. I distinctly remember the day I decided I was going to make that one work, and I was used to being able to *effort* my way through life to get what I wanted. When we had been dating for a year and he hadn't yet told me he loved me, I – once again – forced the issue. Rather than seeing that as some really valuable information, I instead gave him an ultimatum. Of course, he obliged, and I began building our lives together.

My first husband and I rarely fought, but we didn't take the time to connect with each other either. Because he didn't require me to share much of my soul with him, I could stay safe and hidden for many years, but I was not necessarily in love.

During that time, I was so preoccupied with making my life *look* picture-perfect that I wasn't actually living it. I was in corporate marketing and I was an overachiever, constantly searching for that next promotion, that next job, or that next big project. I survived on ego-candy and brought that same controlling energy home at night.

I began noticing other couples that had a natural affection between them, the kind where a hand lands on a leg or a head gently rests on a shoulder. I would notice couples for whom conversation flowed easily and their eyes never left each other. There was a comfort, an ease, and a connectedness between those people that was so foreign to me, but that made my heart ache and made me long for more in my own relationship.

I didn't know how to have that with someone, and neither did my husband. We were both many things at that time, but we were not intimate and vulnerable with each other.

If I could have created a checklist for my husband to do each day to make me feel loved and adored, he would have tried to do those things and checked off every box dutifully. But I didn't know how to ask for whatever was missing, or how to receive it, or how to give it. The longing and loneliness I felt became increasingly present, until it was a big, gaping hole in the center of my heart.

I did my best to convince myself that my husband had enough other good qualities and I just needed to learn to live without affection and connection. And that worked for a while; until it didn't.

After eleven years, my marriage to this good, kind man ended.

A dear friend, someone who is like a father to me recently asked, "Could you have made it work?"

I said, "That's a bit of a loaded question. I could have made it work. I could have continued to suppress who I was and what I longed for. I could have stayed in a small, safe box – continuing to numb and distract myself from the sharp edges of my life. I could have remained a victim and blamed him for my unhappiness, never looking at my role in it. But if I had, I would not know what I know today about how true connection and intimacy only comes from allowing truth to rise to the surface. I would not have been able to become the woman I am today inside of that marriage."

Our Role in the Creation of Our Experiences

When I was in my first marriage and facing the *Why isn't this enough?* question myself, I had some soul-searching to do. I began where it felt easy: by blaming my husband. I created a story in my mind that he couldn't love me the way I needed to be loved. I told myself that I wanted something he couldn't give. There is some truth to that, but that's not the full story.

I knew who he was when I met him. He was the one who was safe and secure. He was also reserved and structured. He was the guy every parent would want their daughter to marry. I ignored the fact that there was very little spontaneity or passion in his life and in our relationship. I didn't question the absence of those ingredients. I did what I was supposed to do, hid my heart, kept myself distracted, kept myself from getting hurt. I made that trade-off and, to a certain degree, it served me.

Eleven years later, he was still the same kind, good, responsible man I married.

To find some healing, I had to own my part in the creation of my experience.

At Some Level, We Knew

When I'm meeting with a new client for the first time, I always ask them about their relationship when they first met and when they got married. Although how they felt about their husband at that time is different than how they feel about him today, it's not uncommon for them to express to me that, on some level, they knew. Many women have shared with me that, even on the day they were walking down the aisle, they knew they might be making a mistake.

My client Gabriele had been married for twelve years to her husband Dalton. She still had love for Dalton; he was a good father, he was optimistic, and he was fun to be around. But there had been one battle in their marriage that happened over and over and over again: He made big financial decisions without consulting her, leaving her feeling nervous and untrusting of him.

Gabriele and I had been working together for a few months before she shared an important story with me. The week Gabriele and Dalton returned from their honeymoon, they had a big discussion and made an agreement with each other that neither was ever going to spend more than $500 without talking to the other one first.

The stakes in their lives aren't $500 anymore; sometimes they're tens or even hundreds of thousands of dollars, but the problem remains. She didn't realize that not everyone feels the need to sit down, have a conversation, and make an agreement like they did, that with many couples it's understood that you make big financial decisions together. At some level, even the week after her honeymoon, she knew she needed to have that conversation with her husband. She knew she needed to say out loud and have him agree that he wouldn't do the very thing she feared most that he would do.

Another client, Alison, told me the story about how she and her husband wrote letters to each other to read on the day of their wedding before walking down the aisle. She can't remember exactly what she wrote or what his letter specifically said to her, but she distinctly remembers thinking, back there in the little room in the back of the church, "He loves me more than I love him."

Even then, on their wedding day, at some level, she knew.

Chapter 3:

The Truth about the Life You Envisioned

"Comparison is a slippery slope to envy...."

DANIELLE LAPORTE

We come into this world as perfect clean slates. From the minute we're born, we begin to learn from those around us. We know how to get mom's attention and we know what not to do so dad doesn't get upset. We learn certain values along the way that define for us who we should be and how we should behave. Likewise, that defines for us who others should be and gives us a framework for what's right and wrong, good and bad. And those values in the context of that framework guide our actions and choices.

Most of what we can envision for ourselves is based upon what we've seen and experienced at home growing up. We know what love and marriage look like by watching mom and dad interact with one another. We know what a family is supposed to look like based upon how we grew up and how others in our neighborhoods and in our schools behaved and what they said. Through social and cultural influences, we create the way we think and believe life *should be*.

It's a rare one of us who can see a future that includes something we've never seen anyone ever do or have before.

For many of us, we do our best to live into that life that we think we should have; learning to ignore, or at least side-step for a while, what feels good for us or what is actually possible.

The White-Picket-Fence Myth

When Sandy and David started out in their marriage they did what most of us did. They established themselves in their careers, they bought a home, and then within a few years began having children. Their lives centered around their jobs, taking care of the kids, and taking care of their home. Their free time was spent with neighbors who cultivated their own versions of the "white picket fence dream"—everyone leading the same suburban existence and no one ever letting on that there was something missing in their lives. It's like a pact that if we stick together, we can collectively convince ourselves that this life we have created is enough.

As their kids grew older, they signed them up for multiple sport and other classes. The kids wanted to play football, soccer, and run track, while Sandy wanted them to learn how to play the piano and participate in church activities with other kids. She became the shuttle driver, in addition to the corporate executive, the good wife, the perfect mother, and the house manager. She made sure the kids' clothes were washed, their favorite snacks were in the cabinet, and their homework was completed before bedtime.

Meanwhile, her marriage was on autopilot. And tending to that just seemed like one more thing that never quite made it to the top of her list.

As the children grew older and became increasingly independent, Sandy had time to focus more on her career. She began to excel at work, receiving promotions and discovering a new joy for her work that she hadn't been able to appreciate previously. With that success came longer hours at the office and more confidence in herself. With that increased level of confidence came a new sense of self. With that comfort in her own skin came attention from men. Something was shifting in her, but David didn't notice.

David was fine with *fine*. He was fine with a marriage that wasn't overflowing with passion, because they had a family together. He was fine with working hard and staying late at the office, because taking care of the family financially was his way of showing love. David was fine with not talking as much and with having sex less and less, because he knew how tired both he and Sandy were at the end of most days. He loved his wife. He loved his family. He liked his job, and he didn't really have desires for more. He was fine with *fine*.

But Sandy did want more in her life: more connection, more experiences, more passions that made her feel alive. She used to want *fine*; she even vaguely remembers a time when she was simply too tired for anything but *fine*. But Sandy was no longer fine with *fine*. No one had ever told us that the life she'd envisioned might not be enough at some point.

Picture Perfect

We live in an interesting time of sharing snippets of happiness on social media while assuming we're seeing everyone else's whole picture. And so we make assumptions that keep us feeling like we're not measuring up.

My client Theresa compared her life to those of her Facebook friends' and was convinced that their lives were clearly better than hers.

She didn't take exotic vacations; she was lucky to even have a day off.

Her kids didn't look like they just came out of a magazine shoot; most of the time they were running and yelling and had spilled something on their shirts... again.

She also didn't have an obviously loving relationship like the couple celebrating their eighteenth wedding anniversary clearly had; she felt like she and her husband had become, on good days, decent co-parents, and on the bad days, quarreling roommates.

Here's the problem: You can't compare the totality of your life and marriage to the small and carefully selected morsels of others' lives and marriages. On most days, it's difficult enough to know what's real and true in our own lives, much less anyone else's.

My marriage to my first husband *looked* picture-perfect, while I *felt* numb and alone.

Lynne's marriage to her husband the pediatrician *looked* like a dream from the outside, but she *felt* lost and drained inside.

And we're not the only ones who have experienced this.

We live in a time where we shout from the rooftops all that is good in our lives and hide the rest in the shadows. We don't talk about the challenges and we end up feeling like we're all alone, the only one feeling this way. That's a slippery slope to thinking we're somehow broken (while everyone else is whole and happy); that there's something wrong with us (that no one else contends with).

We think that by showing only the façades of our lives, we will be able to escape judgment and criticism from others... but maybe it's the judgment and criticism from ourselves that we most fear.

We judge each other based upon what we see, even when what we see is never the full story.

We bought into an idea of what life was supposed to look like that was based on what we saw previously.

We made some choices based upon unsupported beliefs about what was really possible.

We then use that as a weapon against ourselves as proof that we're broken, lost, or alone. We judge ourselves and then try to hide to avoid the judgment from everyone else. But hiding keeps us in fear. Hustling for approval leaves us empty. And denying our hearts, our voices, and our needs just leaves us exhausted.

Go Easy...

As I think back to the time in my life when I felt like I had to hide and hustle, there was one pivotal event that changed me and allowed me to choose a different way of being: I wrote my memoir. My commitment in that book was to be completely honest and open and authentic about my past, my pain, and my journey.

As my first book, it wasn't particularly well-written, but it played an important role in my life. Once I'd told the truth to myself and I published it to share with everyone else, I had no more need or ability to hide from what was real and true for me. I didn't have to hide anymore because I had shared everything I was so afraid people would find out. I had looked at my own darkness and owned it, and maybe even extended some love and grace to it a little bit.

Yes, I was judged for some of the things I wrote about in that book. And sometimes that judgment stung, but it never stung as bad as the pain of the constant struggle to hide who I was and to not own my own life.

The world didn't crumble.

The sun still rose the next day.

I was judged and life moved on.

But it moved on in the light of day, in the light of love, rather than in the shadow of fear.

The other important thing I found at the end of writing and publishing a memoir was that when I saw the woman who had walked through that fire, who had faced her fears, who had most certainly not done everything *right*, and who had often made life far more difficult than it needed to be… I kind of liked her. She was and is a pretty special soul and, for the first time in my life, I wanted to take care of her, I wanted her light to shine brightly, I wanted her to know that she would never have to hide again.

You don't have to write and publish a memoir to gain all the same insights; you just have to get honest with yourself and with everyone else about who you are and what you want in this precious life.

You just have to bring your heart out of hiding.

You just have to love all those crazy imperfections.

You just have to make the conscious choice to take off the armor you think is protecting you.

You just have to drop the mask and let people see you.

You just have to be willing to walk away from people (or let them leave, as the case may be) who don't celebrate you – all of you, the whole of you.

You just need to extend the same love and grace to yourself that you wish others would extend to you.

Go easy on yourself. Go easy on others. We're all doing the best we can to carve out some happiness in this precious life.

Chapter 4:

The Truth about Why You're Not Happy

"How happy you are in any moment is equal to the amount of love you are allowing..."

TRACI SNYDER

Most of us live fairly conditional lives. We are happy when things are going our way and unhappy when things are falling apart. That's how our parents lived, that's what our friends do, and, in my opinion, that is a natural reaction.

When your husband does what he says he was going to do, you feel happy (or at least not irritated).

When your kids are thriving in school and getting good grades, that makes you happy.

When the scale shows a number that you like, you feel good.

But when things aren't going our way, we don't see any possible way to be happy.

My husband forgot my birthday.

My child is grounded for talking back to me.

That darn scale…

We react to what's happening around us, without giving any thought or effort to what's happening within us.

We can live that way, but it's uncomfortable. We're batted around throughout the day based upon who we interact with and what kind of day *they're* having. It leaves us feeling powerless and at the mercy of everyone around us. And we feel resentful since, clearly, some people just got lucky in life and get to live happily ever after and we don't.

We can stay there, but it will never feel good. We will believe that we don't have much control over our lives and how we feel. And feeling powerless never feels good.

Once we begin to see how our experiences don't just happen *to* us, but also *through* us, we can feel more in control of our lives.

A Note about Feeling

Everything we want – a nice home, a good marriage, thriving children, good health, more money – every single thing we want we want because of how we believe we will *feel* when we have it.

I want a nice home so that I feel like I have a sanctuary, somewhere to go that's comforting and peaceful.

I want a good marriage because love feels really good.

I want thriving children because I will feel proud.

I want good health because it will make me feel strong.

I want more money because it will be so fun to spend it or it will make me feel safe (if you're a saver, rather than a spender).

So, ultimately, what we're in pursuit of is what we want to experience feeling: happy, alive, strong, proud, safe, peaceful, fun, excited, adventurous, at ease, healthy, loving, loved, etc. We can sum that up as *feeling good*. We all want to feel good in as many ways as possible.

Let's Make This Real

I'm going to do my best to not make this sound like life-coachy rainbows and unicorns and instead, connect the dots for you in a very real way.

My client Alison had been married to Brandon for fourteen years. She was a successful human resources director and a mother of two children. Between work, her kids, the home, and family, her needs never made it to the top of her list. Over time, what she wanted became unimportant and went unexpressed. Because she was the ultimate multitasker, she took care of everything: grocery shopping, laundry, cooking, homework, baths, sleepovers and birthday parties, hiring people, firing people, helping people grow in their careers, family vacations, cookouts and holiday parties. (Although she never said it, I'm pretty sure she could also leap tall buildings in a single bound.)

She taught people (through her actions and priorities) that her needs weren't important. *She* did that.

She demonstrated to her husband that she didn't need anyone, that she could do it all. But then she resented him for not seeing that she was struggling and felt exhausted.

No one was taking care of her. No one was making sure that, at the end of the day, she was feeling good. But it wasn't anyone else's job to take care of her or to make her feel good. It was her job to take care of herself in a way that helped her to feel good so that she had something to give. Until she realized that, she would continually look to everyone around her to do for her what she could only do for herself.

As long as she kept looking outside of herself, the distance between her and Brandon would continue to grow wider. And then she would carry the stories that *Brandon doesn't care about my happiness, he doesn't care about my needs, and he doesn't take care of me.*

That's not Brandon's job. It's Alison's job.

Alison didn't come into this world with the life mission of taking care of everyone else and totally neglecting herself (although, as a mother, she's certainly received enough messages to the contrary). She didn't come into this world to force others to do what she wanted so she could feel happy.

Her soul came into this world to learn and expand and grow and enjoy. She has a purpose that is all her own and gifts to share, for sure. She came to pursue the desires placed in her heart, and to love and be loved. When she's living in that way, she feels good. Her journey is supposed to feel good.

You Can Only Create in Your Own Experience

If you're with me so far, on the idea that, for most of us, we've been reacting to what's happening around us and letting that dictate our level of happiness…

And if you're with me on the idea that we want what we want because of how we will feel when we have it…

And if you're with me on the idea that, mostly, we just want to feel good (i.e., happy)…

Then you're ready to be exposed to the concept that no one else but you can ultimately create in your physical experience – at least, not without your permission.

You are the one who has control over how to guide and direct your life, through the small, daily choices you make. You're the one who reacts to what's happening around you or not happening around you. You're the one who chooses to read a book or turn on CNN. You're the one who determines who you give your time, energy, or heart to. You're the one who allows either toxic and harmful or inspiring and supportive people into your life.

All of those people and situations leave you feeling either good or bad.

So, ultimately, you're the only one who can be responsible for how you feel.

This doesn't mean that when someone hurts you, you should just be happy about that (that's unicorns and rainbows); but that betrayal does provide you with some really valuable information and gives you some choices to make so that you don't experience that same hurt repeatedly. It might mean you need to set some healthier boundaries. It might mean it's time to communicate and express what you need. It might mean walking away from a painful relationship.

But it absolutely means that you have far more control in your life, your happiness, and your ability to feel good than you might have previously believed.

The Decision to Be Happy

Here's the opportunity that's available to us – to all of us: We can make the *decision* to be happy.

And we can take intentional action to do the things that make us feel good.

By default, that might mean pruning away the people and experiences that don't feel good.

If we have ten topics in our lives (money, health, work, kids, marriage, etc.) and nine of those topics are going really well, we can choose to look at and pay attention to those nine things, or we can choose to focus on the one thing that's not going as well. Often, we think that by our focus and attention on the one thing that's falling apart, we'll be able to figure it out or beat it into submission. But when the ultimate goal is to be happy and to feel good, we might want to make a different choice for ourselves and look around, instead, at all the things that are going well.

"So, keep my head in the sand? Ignore reality? But what's happening is true! It's really not going well!"

Yeah... maybe.

As my favorite spiritual teacher, Abraham-Hicks, has taught me, there are lots of things that are true. You can choose to look at the thing that's true that feels good when you look at it and focus on it (your kid giving you a big hug, something you recently accomplished, or getting a good night's rest). Or you can look at the thing that doesn't feel good when you think about it and focus upon it (your husband forgetting your birthday or making big decisions without you or even the fact that he hasn't said "I love you" in at least a year).

It's all a choice.

When you set the simple but profound intention that you want to feel good, you'll be amazed at how that impacts who is in your life and how you spend your time and energy. You'll see your choices shift. Some of your choices might even seem irresponsible or selfish. That's okay. When feeling good is your highest intention and you deliver that promise to yourself, you're a better mother, a better wife, a better friend, and a better woman.

Chapter 5:

The Truth about What to Do About It

"Some of the biggest challenges in relationships come from the fact that most people enter a relationship in order to get something: they're trying to find someone who's going to make them feel good."

ANTHONY ROBBINS

There could be any number of reasons why you picked up this book at this particular time in your life and in your marriage:

- Maybe the distance between you and your husband has become too unbearable.
- Maybe you wake up every day thinking, "I can make this work," but then fall asleep at night thinking to yourself, "I can't do this one more day."
- Maybe the weight of the guilt you've been carrying about not loving a man who should be so perfectly loveable has begun to pull you under.
- Maybe you're so exhausted from keeping up the appearances of this perfect marriage that you find yourself simply going through the motions each day.
- Maybe there's even been something that's woken you up to the question, Why isn't this enough?

You know a bit more now than you did before you picked up this book. You know how you got to this point in your life. And I suppose I could have written an entire book on forgiving yourself for past choices or making better decisions moving forward. Even if I had, the truth is that you can't go back.

This is where you are. And you're exactly where you're supposed to be. You haven't done anything wrong. Your experience is completely valid. Don't judge yourself for the way you feel.

No one teaches us this stuff. We didn't learn about it in school. We didn't learn it from watching others. And most of us didn't learn it from our parents. There's no manual out there to tell each of us the one way to navigate our most intimate relationships so that we avoid pain and stay in a state of love forever.

But there is something you can do about where you are now. And you don't have to blow up your life. You don't have to become a completely different person. You don't have to become an alcoholic or a heroin addict. There is a sane way to feel better.

These Problems Don't Typically Age Well

When left unattended, the questions in our marriages of *Why isn't this enough?* and *Why am I unhappy?* typically don't age well. If you do nothing, you will very likely be in the same place or a worse place at this time next year, two years from now, and ten years from now.

Things don't magically get better. As a matter of fact, things tend to get worse. The problem won't fix itself. You can't change something that you're not willing to look at. And you can't learn from something you ignore.

A house that's not lived in deteriorates at a much faster rate than a home that's lived in and cared for.

Your Journey (Not Mine)

This work is hard. It just is.

I know because I've been there and I guide women through it every day.

That's why most people don't do it – because it's hard. That's why most stay stuck. That's why so many are so unhappy. And knowing that is why your story will be different.

Throughout the next three sections of this book, I'm going to help guide you from where you are now to where you can go from here. That route will likely be a different path than you've taken before.

I have no agenda for your life. I'm not going to attempt to save your marriage for you. Nor do I believe that every marriage should last forever. I'm here to guide you through *your* journey.

There's not a reason in the world why your journey has to look like my journey. I did it the long and painful way. And that's why I've now dedicated my life to guiding others along a more peaceful and loving path.

No Mud, No Lotus

The lotus flower emerges from murky, muddy ponds, breaking the surface of the water each morning and blooming. It doesn't grow from well-fertilized soil or in pots that have been cared for by loving hands. It rises from the darkness, it materializes from mud, it emerges new each morning and blooms again.

Whatever you've done in your past that you regret, leave it down there in the muddy waters.

Whatever pain you've experienced, know that it is shaping you into the person you are today… and into who you will be tomorrow.

Whatever fears you carry, know that each day is a new opportunity to turn your face toward the light and bloom.

If there was no mud, there would be no lotus.

Want more Soulful Truth Telling?

Get any of my free ebooks
on love and relationships:
SharonPopeGoodness.com

Section Two:

Where Are You Now?

Chapter 6:

The Truth about Your Marriage Today

"Everything that irritates us about others can lead us to an understanding of ourselves."

CARL JUNG

There's likely a part of you that wants to make this marriage work and a part of you that's ready to throw in the towel. I know it would be so much easier if you could just find a way to re-connect with your husband. It would be so much easier if he would just be the man you need him to be. It would be so much easier if you could just stop thinking that there must be something more.

Sand is created over long periods of time, from rocks and minerals in the ocean breaking down into smaller and smaller grains. The constant movement of the ocean and the weathering process contribute to that process of breaking down, which can occur quickly in rough waters or more slowly in calmer waters.

It's the same with our marriages. Sometimes the relationship is tumultuous and it breaks down quickly, but most of the women I speak with live through the weathering process over many years and even decades before realizing their marriage has broken down enough that's it's no longer a stable foundation for anything substantial. The continuous feeling of emptiness chips away at our souls until we realize there's very little left of any substance or value.

None of us set out to enter into a marriage that would eventually leave us feeling empty, numb, or alone. We all went into it with the best of intentions, believing it would last "until death do us part." But slowly, over time, you've changed and the relationship has changed.

We Are Teachers for One Another

Our closest personal relationships are incredibly important to our soul's journey. They are often divine gifts that are meant to present to us the exact lesson we need most and help us step into who we came into this life to become. They are often the greatest source of pain, but also the greatest source of healing in our lives.

The people we marry and commit to spending our lives with will be the ones who teach us the most – mostly about ourselves. That's one of the reasons they're present in our lives. But, as helpful as they are at pressing our buttons, being our mirrors, and presenting us with the lessons we most need to learn, they're equally as helpful at teaching us unconditional love, boundaries, and the importance of self-love.

What I've Learned

Through love, what I've learned about myself is that I have a big heart and a brave spirit. I know that my heart is the most precious gift I can give someone, so only those who deserve it and can treat it with both kindness and respect get a key.

What I've learned about love is that it is, by far, the most powerful force in the universe. We were born from it, we live for it, and, in the end, it's all we're here to do. I've learned that nothing is impossible when love is present.

What I've learned about marriage is that it's a dance. It's not always in step or on time, and it's not always graceful, but when both souls are engaged and paying attention, it can be a lot of fun.

What I've learned is that in my marriage to my amazing husband, Derrick, there are times when I am a passionate lover, a committed friend, and an unwavering partner. There are times when I am strong and times when I am weak. There are times when I am fabulous and flirtatious, and other times when I am messy and magnificent. In my marriage, my husband gets all the parts of me and I get all of the parts of him.

What I've learned about relationships, in general, is that there is a subtle but tremendous difference between effort and force. There's not a single thing wrong with effort. Many good things in our lives come with some effort; there's strength in effort.

But almost nothing good comes from force.

Attempting to use force when it comes to relationships can be painful and grueling, and leaves us feeling weak and defeated. It's the difference between paddling upstream and turning your raft downstream.

The Good in Goodbye

When we realize we are all teachers for one another and every experience we have is just another step on the path of our soul's journey, the significance of our painful relationship experiences soften.

My client Karen got out of a marriage that lasted almost three decades and, although she would admit that she wasn't happy in the marriage, his leaving left her heartbroken, nonetheless. When she was far enough removed from the pain of that relationship, she was able to see that he was in her life to get her to see how she was subjugating all her needs and wants. He was there to push her to the edge, where the truth was staring her in the face: Until she became a priority in her own life, she wouldn't be a priority in anybody else's life either. And she learned that as long as she felt like she had to keep giving and giving and giving, he would drain her through the constant taking and taking and taking. He was there to help her get to a place where she could really love and appreciate her heart and honor her needs and wants.

Since the end of that relationship, Karen's had a few intimate relationships that also presented some important lessons. One man showed her that she was, in fact, desirable and lovable. Another showed her that you can have a man who is strong and protective as well as gentle and kind. She began to embrace who she was and get clear about what she wanted in a relationship.

The Single Biggest Mistake We All Make

There is one single mistake that we make from time to time that is the basis for many of our painful relationship issues. And that is needing the other person to be different so that we can feel better.

I'd like to introduce you to my client Camille. Camille has been married to Joe for 26 years. She has devoted her entire adult life to caring for her family, their home, and their two beautiful daughters. Camille kept herself very busy while the girls were growing up and Joe was building his real estate business. She hadn't realized how distant their marriage had become over the years until she was faced with the emptiness that existed at home when the youngest left for college. She didn't realize how incredibly lonely she had become until it was only her and Joe sitting across the dinner table each night with nothing to discuss.

Camille and Joe hadn't had sex in over five years by then, and she couldn't remember the last time he'd kissed her and told her he loved her. She started wondering if he had ever loved her and she questioned her love for him.

Camille woke-up each day wavering between anxious and lonely, desperately seeking some kind of attention and approval from her husband. She wanted him to see her, to really see her. She wanted him to connect with her, listen to her, and be loving toward her. But that's not who he was. As a matter of fact, that's not who he'd ever been. And she was only just noticing that.

Joe, on the other hand, wanted his good wife back. He wanted the wife who didn't cause ripples, didn't ask for much, and didn't express her needs. He wanted her to be small and quietly supportive of him, without desires and dreams of her own.

It would be easy to debate who was right and who was wrong in that situation, but that's not the point. The point is they were both miserable because they each wanted the other to be or do something that they were not.

Camille found her voice. Now she's not going to go back to being small and quiet with no needs or desires of her own.

Joe is not going to be attentive and loving and intimate with her.

As long as they each need the other to do those things in order to be happy, they will each remain miserable. And they will blame each other for their unhappiness.

Let's Talk about Sex

Since we touched on the topic already, let's go there. It's difficult to talk about healing intimate relationships and not include some discussion on sex within the relationship.

Earlier I introduced you to my client Lynne who is married to the pediatrician. You'll recall that she and James were still sleeping together, but she said it felt like a chore. It felt to her like her husband was one more person who wanted something from her and, by the end of the day, she had nothing left to give. She couldn't remember the last time she'd had an orgasm, although he doesn't know that.

If you've ever watched the *Sex in the City* episode where the character Miranda talks about sex and marriage, you'll know how Lynne felt. She was in that phase where she didn't enjoy sex, she didn't want it to last longer, she just wanted to *get it over with*.

There may be a few exceptions to this rule, but I think it would be very difficult to have a healthy, loving, intimate, connected relationship without the physical piece.

Being physical has to be enjoyable for both people, otherwise it's not sustainable. We simply won't continue doing something that doesn't feel good.

It has to feel safe for both people, an experience where you can both share the most intimate parts of each other without judgment or criticism.

Sex has to be part of the conversation if you're going to figure out a way to make the marriage work.

Chapter 7:

The Truth about Loving Him

"And the lesson is always, in some way, the expansion of our capacity to love."

MARIANNE WILLIAMSON

During the writing of this book, I had a conversation with my writing coach and friend, Angela. We talked about her first marriage and a piece of advice someone gave her that has stuck with her all these years. She was told, "You can't leave him until you love him." At first I didn't quite understand. I couldn't connect the dots. What her friend meant was that until you can accept and see your

49

husband as a whole person, as he truly is, you can't stay and be happy, *but you can't go and be happy either*. Because until you can fully love and accept him, you will carry that wound in your heart into future relationships and it will guide your choices and influence your expectations.

He's Doing the Best He Can

I have a belief that we're all doing the best we can with where we are in our respective journeys. He's not intentionally holding out on you or purposely attempting to torture you. This is who he is and he's doing the best he can.

My client Gabriele who is married to Dalton can't understand why he continues to do the very thing that tears her apart – not including her in large financial decisions – time and again, but then say that he genuinely wants to make the marriage work. Dalton loves his wife; I've never met him, but that I know. He genuinely doesn't understand what she's asking for or how to give it to her. He feels like he's walking on eggshells all the time so that she won't get upset and, in his eyes, overreact. She thinks he disregards her opinion and she doesn't feel like part of a couple. It's like the two of them are speaking in different languages. One is speaking in Italian and the other in Spanish. While there's some crossover between the two, all of the details are lost in translation.

Have you ever had the experience where you saw something happen and you described it one way, but someone else who also saw what happened described it in a totally different way? We can each only see things through our own lens. Embedded in that lens are all the life experiences, beliefs, and judgments that color the way we see things. And since no two people have ever had the exact same life experience or carry the exact same beliefs and feelings about what's right and wrong, no two people can see a single thing in the exact same way.

So often we think that if our partners aren't doing what we would do or what we would want them to do that they're deliberately choosing to not do that for us. We think they should be able to clearly understand our needs and know how to provide them for us, when many times they're simply experiencing the situation through a completely different lens. Most men don't wake up and think, "How can I make my wife mad or miserable today? What could I do (or avoid doing) so that she feels unsupportive, disconnected, and unloved?"

Your husband may just be seeing life through his lens and, frankly, that's all any of us have the equipment to do. On any given day, we're all simply doing the best we can with where we are on our own journey. You may want him to be on a different part of his journey – more evolved, more in touch with his feelings, more communicative – but that's like trying to turn an orange into a kumquat.

We can always evolve further, learn something new, do better when we know better, but for the most part, we're all doing the best we can.

Our Whole Selves

We all have parts of ourselves that are dominant in our experience; these are the things that guide our choices and our lives. Most of those things we would probably judge as good.

For instance, some of the pieces of my primary self are:

- Smart
- Strong
- Generous
- Loving
- Creative

We all also have parts of ourselves that we deny and like to run from – our shadow selves. These are typically aspects we perceive as being not good. They are often the exact opposite of the aspects that compose our primary selves. Running from them doesn't mean they're inactive in us; they're actually the things that influence us most, by sneaking in and showing up in our judgments and fears.

My shadow self (the parts I don't like to admit to) are:

- Dumb
- Weak
- Stingy
- Hateful
- Intellectual

I can be the super-smart business woman and still make mistakes that my father makes blonde jokes about. There are times when I can be strong and courageous, and also weak and scared to death.

Think about a time when you were scared to do something, but you did it anyway. We actually embody both ends of the spectrum that make up our primary and shadow selves. We hide the shadow pieces to avoid our own judgment or the judgment of others.

When we can integrate the shadow parts of ourselves and see how that serves us, we can embrace more of who we are. When we can accept our whole selves, we're able to accept the whole of others – even including the things we consider flaws.

When you can begin to see your husband as a whole person – his primary self *and* his shadow self – you can love him. That doesn't necessarily mean you will make the choice to live happily ever after with him, but you can love him and understand who he is.

Love Is a Choice We Make

We all want that feeling of love to be directed at us; it feels like standing in the sunlight. Like my beloved client Camille, we want our husbands to love us and we want to feel the warmth of that light.

But something we don't give nearly as much thought to is becoming the one who loves, making the choice to love, just because it feels good. No matter how you feel about your relationship in any given moment, love always feels better than hate or fear or anger. Always.

So when you begin to care enough about feeling good to start doing things differently, and you really begin to take responsibility for your own happiness, you make the choice to love – even when it's difficult.

You love because it's the nature of who we are and what we came here to do and experience.

You do it selfishly – for you, not him.

Rather than worrying about his love being focused on you, you become the one who loves.

Love whatever you can, even if it's not him in this particular moment. Love your children, love the smell of fresh cut flowers, love waking up after a good night's rest. Just find something to love.

When we can become the one who loves, we can stop struggling and grasping.

Love is a choice we can make.

It is an action we can take.

To stop loving is to cut off the channel to our soul.

Love in its most pure form is simply demonstrated *through us.*

At the core, love is all we are. And it's all we're here to do.

Chapter 8:

The Truth about Changing Him

"The beginning of love is to let those we love be perfectly themselves, and not to twist them to fit our own image. Otherwise we love only the reflection of ourselves we find in them."

THOMAS MERTON

Janice's husband had been unfaithful to her. More than once. More than twice. He carried on several affairs throughout the last few years of their 19-year marriage and, as a result of the last affair, he not only lost the girlfriend, he lost his job, some close friends, and he almost lost his wife and boys, too.

Janice was absolutely shattered when we spoke for the first time. Over the course of her coaching session she told me about the affairs and how hurt she was. She shared with me that she had threatened to leave her husband and was still considering doing so. She told me her husband was doing everything he knew how to do now in order to save the marriage:

He'd become completely open about where he was, who he was with, and when he would be home. He was home a lot more and he was not on his phone texting endlessly when he was home.

He was engaged with the children and spent lots of quality time with them.

He apologized. He told her at least once a day how beautiful she was and he showered her with love and affection.

He'd even gone back to church.

I remember so clearly the phone call where Janice asked me through her tears, "Can people change? Do you think he's really changed, or am I going to end up back in this same place again?"

Do People Change?

The short answer is, "Yes, people can change." Change is absolutely possible (I'm living proof), but it usually takes us hitting our version of rock-bottom in order to become uncomfortable enough to seek change and be open to a new way.

The long answer is, "We resist change." Change causes discomfort, and we certainly aren't comfortable with discomfort. So the discomfort of our lives has to become greater than the uncomfortableness of change. Janice's husband had clearly become uncomfortable; he almost lost everything.

Unfortunately, if we're not *highly* uncomfortable, we're not going to change for the fun of it and certainly not because someone else wants us to.

When was the last time you tried to get someone to do something they didn't want to do? Did it work?

When was the last time you tried to adopt a new habit and make change in your own life – exercise more, give up caffeine or sugar, show up early to work? Did it become a permanent change? Probably not, because you weren't uncomfortable enough yet. They were things you wanted to do to feel marginally better. The limp desire of wanting to feel marginally better rarely has staying power. However, when the house is burning down around you, you'll make a change or you'll burn up.

Creating Change – What We Can and Cannot Do

You cannot change another soul. You can't make your children like green beans any more than you can make an angry man happy, an unhealthy person healthy, or a hateful man loving. And on any given day, creating change in our own lives is difficult enough. So what in the world makes us think that we can change someone else?

I've found that most women intellectually know this – *you can't change your man* – but that doesn't seem to stop us from trying, does it? I've already told you about the single biggest relationship mistake we all make: *If you would be different, I would feel better.*

- "If you would be more loving toward me, I would feel more loved and desired."
- "If you would believe in me, I would feel more confident in my abilities and be successful."
- "If you would stop criticizing me, I would feel more worthy and accepted."
- "If you would help more with the kids, I would feel more supported."
- "If you would stop being so grouchy all the time, I would be happier."

And that's where the madness begins.

People can change; it's possible. And they may actually become uncomfortable enough in their lives to create lasting change. But you can't do it *for* them. You can only do it for yourself, and only when you really want to.

Gabriele's husband, Dalton, when confronted with a difficult decision or challenging conversation that needs to be had, his tendency is to shut down and avoid it all together. He figures it's easier to ask for forgiveness than permission and he'd rather just take a little nagging from Gabriele than risk having an argument with her. This is what he does: he shuts down, backs away, avoids and ignores the smoldering fire that's sitting there in the middle of the room. Whereas Gabriele wants to talk about the fire: when it started, how it started, what's going to happen if they don't deal with it, and why Dalton hasn't put it out yet. She wants him to talk to her, to open up to her – even when he's upset with her. She wants to be a partner in this relationship; she wants to know what he needs and she wants the opportunity to be heard, as well. She's trying to change him from someone who would rather avoid difficult topics into someone who wants to dive into them.

Dalton is 45 years old and this little characteristic of his has been with him since he was a child. As fabulous and powerful as Gabriele is, she hasn't been able to change him. He hasn't changed when his beloved wife has asked him to again and again and again. He hasn't changed even though it most certainly would cause fewer arguments and would have made life significantly easier. He wouldn't begin to change until he got *really* uncomfortable.

Because this topic is a deal-breaker for Gabriele, she has decided to separate from her husband. She did, and now he's uncomfortable. He's uncomfortable enough that he's at least trying to change. Gabriele didn't leave because she was trying to manipulate him into changing; she left because she felt like without communication the marriage couldn't be salvaged.

At the time of this writing, the jury's still out on whether or not Gabriele and Dalton's marriage will survive. The distance between them may have become too far to bridge. The jury's still out on whether or not Dalton will open up to Gabriele and begin communicating significantly more.

But at least now he's trying.

Chapter 9:

The Truth about the Magic Pill

"What is uttered from the heart alone, will win the hearts of others to your own."

JOHANN WOLFGANG VON GOETHE

I n Chapter Four, you learned that you can't create in anyone's experience but your own.

Now you know (*really know*) that the only person you can ever change is yourself.

Here's how I know that's true: If I could take away my client's pain, sadness, and emptiness, *I would do it.*

One of the things I do with prospective clients is get on a call with them to see if it's a fit for us to work together. I want to work with people who are committed to creating change in their lives and in their most important relationships, and they need to know they can trust and work with a coach, with me, before they can invest in and believe in the process.

One of the clues I use to let me know that a prospective client and I aren't a fit to work together is if they think I have something that I call the *magic pill.* Some people think I have a secret that I can quickly tell them or some magic I can weave to unravel four decades of struggle in 60 minutes. Although I'm pretty magical, I can't do that. And if it was that easy, it would have been figured out and put on the market by now. You'd see that magic pill for sale in Target.

Believe me, if I could provide a magic pill that would make all that you have feel like enough in your marriage, *I would do it.*

If I could give you a lobotomy for that part of your brain that carries all the regret and pain from past relationships, *I would do it.*

If I could give you a simple secret to a happy and loving marriage, *I would do it.*

I would be rich and my clients would be instantly happy again. Everyone wins!

But that's not the way it works. I can't create in your physical experience any more than you can create in your husband's.

Yes, I can guide you.

Yes, I can equip you with tools you didn't have before.

Yes, I can teach you and challenge you and inspire you, but I am unable to create for you.

If there was a magic pill, honestly, I would have found it years ago when I was going through this myself.

This journey you're in that we call life, is yours to do.

Everyone Gets There as They Should

I often pray to my angels to reach out to the women who need me. I ask those angels to have me cross their paths when they're ready for me. Many times I've asked people how they found me and it's not uncommon for me to hear, "I have no idea. You somehow landed in my email or on my Facebook feed." But, I know how it happened. And why. It happened because they were ready.

I don't often have the opportunity to coach men, but I love it when I do. I wish men would tap in to my coaching services a bit more than they do, because after speaking with thousands of women about their relationships, I know a thing or two about what makes women unhappy in their relationships with men and how to make it better.

William contacted me in complete denial. His wife had left a year ago, the marriage officially ended two months ago, and she was dating another man who she loved and wanted to be in their children's lives. William's wife had been his high school sweetheart and she was the mother of his children and he still loved her deeply. When we talked about what had been keeping him stuck, he shared with me that he had spent the past year trying to rebuild the relationship, to no avail. He couldn't believe their challenges were insurmountable or that she no longer loved him.

Obviously, if I had that magic pill and a magic wand, I would bring his wife back to him and hand out the pills. But instead what I offered was a path to healing and growth so that, no matter what happened, he could become the kind of man he wished he had been before his marriage crumbled. He could become a man he was proud to be and a father his kids were proud of.

William didn't hire me as his coach. Maybe that's because he wasn't ready. Maybe that's because he genuinely wanted to keep his pain a little longer. Maybe he found someone he thought could help him more. It's all okay. We can't hear or take in something we're not yet ready to receive. Everyone comes to healing in their own time, in their own way. And it's all okay.

My coach (yes, coaches have coaches) once asked me, "How many times did you have to say 'no' to help and healing before you said 'yes'?" My answer: "Too many to count."

There are many paths to the truth. There's no one right way or wrong way. I believe that the people who find me are those who need me most and the people who invest in themselves through working with me are ready walk into their truth and claim their own life.

Can a Troubled Marriage Be Saved?

Natalie's marriage is on the ropes. She and her husband, Chad, are living apart, they've filed the paperwork, and the divorce process is underway. But she's still not sure if she can walk away from more than two decades with the man she pledged to love forever. They haven't had an emotional connection for a long time, and she never felt heard or beautiful or desired by him in the relationship, but there's still a voice inside her that that whispers, "Is there some way to save this?"

There are a lot of things about Natalie's marriage that didn't work, clearly, since they've gotten this far into the process. She wants an intimate, emotionally connected, and passionate love.

She wants to feel special, heard, and desired in her relationship. She wants to feel alive again.

But there are also a lot of ways that their relationship does work (otherwise she would have left earlier and wouldn't be asking the question). Natalie and Chad always had a lot of fun together and, when they make the space for that, there is always laughter and joy. He's an amazing father and they do a great job of parenting the children together, and have very similar approaches. When she envisioned growing old with someone, it was always with him.

There are also some things that *aren't* working in the *relationship* that *are* working for *Natalie* (stay with me here). Natalie says that she and Chad are disconnected, but it feels safe and comfortable to stay tucked into a story so that she doesn't have to open herself up and be vulnerable with her husband. Staying in that story is actually working for Natalie.

Natalie had planned a romantic long weekend away for the two of them a few months ago and Chad declined, saying he had to work late. That left Natalie feeling rejected and undesirable. That perceived rejection created resentment and a wider gap of disconnection. It's far easier to stay in that rejection-and-disconnection story than to face potential rejection again and attempt to re-connect with her distant husband.

There are pieces of most relationships that work and other pieces that don't. But there are also pieces that don't really work, but are somehow serving you. And *those* are the pieces that are difficult for you to see, because you don't have the same perspective as someone outside of the relationship.

If Natalie can shift her perspective, the marriage might heal. If she stops looking to her husband to change for her and she begins to change for herself, he will either come along for the ride or he won't. Either way, she will grow, she will evolve, and she will live.

Nature as Our Teacher

Nature can be such a beautiful teacher for us. In particular, trees provide a beautiful metaphor for our relationships sometimes.

When a tree is struggling, sometimes it can be saved by pruning away the dying branches, giving it new life so it can thrive once again.

Even when a tree is dying, sometimes it can be rejuvenated by cutting it all the way down to its stump. It's been said that when a fire occurs in a forest, it actually does something to the soil that causes the area to be more conducive to fertile growth.

Sometimes that which is dying can be saved.

But it takes a pruning away of all the parts that no longer serve the relationship, such as:

- The need for our spouse to change who they are in order for us to feel good.
- The story that it's our husband's responsibility for making us feel loved and confident, secure and happy.
- The lie that you can't have a relationship filled with passion and peace, strength and gentleness.

Of course, not everything that's dying can be saved.

Some conditions don't allow the tree to re-blossom.

Some relationships are on life support and too far gone.

And some have been dead a long time already.

Not everything that's dying can be saved; but every relationship can be used to promote new growth. Each fall when the leaves on the trees change color and fall to the ground, something new is being created. Sometimes the gift of letting go allows us to make room for something new.

Chapter 10:

The Truth about Acting Out

"Every woman is a rebel."

OSCAR WILDE

When we're in pain and we feel stuck or trapped in that pain, we can get a little rebellious. When we're frustrated by the painful parts of our marriage, we can start doing things we don't normally do. And it's a cry for help, in its own way.

Juli had been feeling disconnected from her husband for a long time. He didn't know what was wrong. He just knew she had been going out with her friends more often and drinking

71

more wine than usual. He didn't realize that she was numbing and distracting herself in order to avoid feeling the loneliness in their relationship.

Juli started to resent that her husband wasn't noticing the disconnect, wasn't acknowledging her pain, and didn't seem to mind when she spent time with friends rather than him. She wanted him to notice. She wanted him to make it better. She wanted to feel desired and adored by him again.

And that resentment only made things worse.

Going out with girlfriends turned into a girls' trip to Vegas for the weekend.

The girls' trip to Vegas led to kissing someone she didn't even know and never saw again.

That indiscretion led to sending a Facebook message to an old boyfriend to see if the flame between them had fizzled. It hadn't.

That led to her heart longing for someone else... and more bricks were added to the wall she had built around her heart about her husband and her marriage.

And all of that led to a marriage in trouble.

I've seen versions of Juli's story over and over, so I know it occurs far more often than we speak about openly. And I can relate to it because I had my own version of Juli's story in my first marriage. All along the way, at every step, our resentment and acting out was a cry for help, but we felt those feelings and took those actions without ever really expressing what we needed.

The Brokenness Happened Years Ago

Addison and Mason had been married for seventeen years and had three children together, two boys and a girl. He was a farmer and she cared for the children. When the children were young and Addison was doing all she could to get through the days with all the kids in one piece and her sanity intact, Mason decided to take a second job. He began working more evenings and weekends. That left Addison alone, overwhelmed, and lonely.

They didn't see each other much. Mostly they communicated in passing about the kids and what they each needed on a practical level to keep things going. When he came home, he was tired, so he couldn't help much with the kids or the upkeep of the home, and he was too tired to talk or connect. He was doing what he had learned was his role: to provide for his family. None of it was right or wrong, but it told a vivid story of how Addison and Mason got to this place. The divide and distance between them grew over the years. When I asked her how she felt she said, "Frustrated, lost, and broken."

It probably won't surprise you to know that Addison found herself in an emotional and physical affair in which she felt seen and heard. She felt loved and alive again. And they fell in love, so it was complex.

Addison and Mason tried a marriage intensive and counseling and, although Mason was able to see how it had happened, he had not only lost trust in his wife, he couldn't find the way back into her heart again.

Addison didn't want to create a problem. She didn't want to upset her kids or hurt Mason. She didn't want to move out or to break up the family. But she also didn't know how to flip the switch in her heart so that she could fall back in love with her husband.

Let's Blame the Other Man

Many times, our partner's first inclination when cheating, having affairs, and general acting out has occurred is to blame the other guy, the man you had the affair with.

- "If it wasn't for him, you would still be here with me."
- "If it wasn't for him, I wouldn't feel so hurt and betrayed."
- "If it wasn't for him, our marriage wouldn't be crumbling."

But the reality is that the marriage was in trouble long before the affair occurred. Otherwise, it wouldn't have even been a possibility.

When you are deeply in love with your husband, being with someone else isn't an option; it's not even something you think about. It's not that you're not out looking for it, it's that your energy says to everyone around you, "I'm good already. I'm really good."

The marriage was broken far before these women began acting out in various ways. These women, at various times, in various ways, were crying out for help, but either they weren't saying what needed to be heard clearly enough or he wasn't listening.

Acting Out and Self-Sabotage Come in Many Forms

Casey had been working out for a few weeks and she had started feeling pretty good about herself, even though she hadn't begun losing weight yet. She began making snarky comments to her husband when he would eat or drink things that she considered off-limits for her. She was unconsciously blaming him for her not yet losing weight. Those comments she made created a wedge between the two of them and, because it didn't make him feel good about himself, he stopped initiating sex.

His lack of interest in sex made her feel unattractive and the toxic cycle continued for several weeks before she realized what was happening and course-corrected the behavior that had started the cycle in the first place.

Diane had a supportive and loyal husband, but he didn't want to sit down and connect with her. He didn't know her joys or her fears. He didn't know what she was looking forward to or what she dreaded. She knew how to get his attention though. If she wanted his attention, she would go out and buy something that was big enough that he would question it; it would at least get him talking, even if it was yelling. She didn't care about the $5,000 handbag she'd bought. She was crying out for her husband's attention.

Bethany's marriage was too much to face most nights, so she chose to stay at work until late so she wouldn't have to face her husband's sad, longing eyes or have yet another discussion about what wasn't working for her in the relationship.

Acting out in our marriage can take many forms: cheating, eating too much, or bullying and judging other people. It can take the form of spending our way through the pain or working long, long hours to avoid the truth of what waits at home. It's all valid. It's all real. It's all different versions of a cry for help.

- A cry of "Please see me."

- A cry of "Please hear me."
- A cry of "Please acknowledge me."
- A cry of "Please connect with me again and make me feel like I matter."
- A cry of "Please take away this pain."

If some of this sounds familiar to you, understand that all of your actions are a cry for help in some way. Rather than self-imploding or heading down a path where there's no return, it might be easier to just actually cry out for help. Wave the white flag, sound an alarm, do whatever you have to do to express what you need in your marriage and what's hurting your heart.

Marriages end long before they actually end. Marriages grow apart slowly over time. There are opportunities all along the way to notice when you're on the rumble strip on the highway. They caution you to pay attention, long before you land in the ditch.

Want more Soulful Truth Telling?

Get any of my free ebooks
on love and relationships:
SharonPopeGoodness.com

Section Three:

The Answers Within

Chapter 11:

The Truth about Forgiving Yourself

"Forgiveness does not change the past, but it does enlarge the future."

PAUL BOOSE

Juli, who found herself in an affair at one point in her marriage, carried tremendous guilt and shame about her actions and choices.

- How could I have allowed it to get that far?
- What kind of person does that?
- My husband deserves so much better than that.

Although she was no longer seeing the man she had the affair with, she couldn't seem to escape the brokenness she felt as a result. She didn't want to justify it or blame anyone else, but she also didn't want to live with such intense sadness.

Addison fell in love with another man.

Casey was unkind to her husband when she was struggling with her weight.

Diane spent too much money as a means of getting her husband's attention.

I doubt there is anyone walking our planet today that doesn't have something in their past that they regret or that they might want to do differently if given the opportunity. But it never feels good to bring your past into your present. Here's why:

- Focusing on the past robs you of the present that is available to you and the chance to be in alignment with who you really are now.
- It will always feel worse to relive painful past memories, because you have even less control over that issue now than you did at the time.

So it's not only unproductive, it keeps you stuck in the past, unable to move forward.

What is Forgiveness?

Forgiveness, at its core, is the intentional act of releasing resentments toward people who have wronged us or caused us pain – even if that person is ourselves.

Forgiveness is not the same as admitting defeat, showing weakness, or saying that what someone did was okay.

The weight of regret and judgment is like carrying a 20-pound weight around your neck everywhere you go. And you're the only one who can take that weight off; no one else can do it for you. You're the keeper of the keys to your own prison.

Loving, Accepting, and Forgiving Ourselves

The work of forgiveness begins by going within, because it is only once we can love, accept, and forgive ourselves that we're able to love, accept, and forgive those we're closest to.

Whatever you're judging yourself for, there's a reason why you did it. Maybe you did it for some relief, as an escape from the sharp edges of your life. Maybe you didn't know what you didn't know or you weren't paying attention. Or maybe you were acting on the outside how you were feeling inside – full of anger, sadness, or inner turmoil.

Maybe you just wanted to feel loved.

It's time that you finally forgive yourself.

- Forgive yourself for not knowing what you didn't know.
- Forgive yourself for not seeing what you didn't see.
- Forgive yourself for abandoning your heart and/or your needs and/or your voice.
- Forgive yourself for what you overlooked.
- Forgive yourself for not telling yourself the truth.
- Forgive yourself for not telling others the truth.
- Forgive yourself for thinking you could change someone.
- Forgive yourself for not asking questions because you didn't want to hear the answers.
- Forgive yourself for not treating others in a way that aligns with your values.
- Forgive yourself for all of it.

No Harsher Critic

We are a world of people who judge each other. Although none of us would like to think of ourselves as judgmental, it's all around us. We judge other mothers and how they parent. We judge people who are of different religious backgrounds so that we can feel more right or righteous. We judge gays, lesbians, men, other women, Blacks, Hispanics, people we work with, people who cut us off in traffic, our parents, our friends… you name it and we judge it. But even with as cruel as we can be to one another, oftentimes, no one judges us more harshly than we judge ourselves.

We say things to ourselves that we would never say to our daughters or our best friends. And we will carry a judgment about ourselves far longer than it would take for us to forgive someone who wronged us in some way.

We carry that burden because we don't want to let ourselves off the hook – but also because sometimes we're scared that if we put that weight down, we might still do the same thing again. We don't trust ourselves to do better. But, in the words of Maya Angelou, "Once you know better, you do better."

Now That You Know

You now know something you didn't know previously. And once you know something, you can't un-know it. You can't unlearn what you've learned about yourself.

Our experiences change us, so there is no going backwards. Even if you wanted to, even if you hadn't been paying attention, you won't do that thing again (whatever it is you're beating yourself up about), because the discord of it would feel even worse than it did the first time. You can forgive yourself, but there's a part of you that won't forget how that felt. So trust yourself that next time will be different; that your future will look different than your past.

I've told you I'm a big believer in the idea that we're all doing the best we can with where we are in our journey. You were doing the best you could at that point in your life. You're in a different place now. Next time will be different because you're different.

I Deserve This

Lynne was struggling about not appreciating all that she had. You may recall that she was married to a pediatrician who loved her, she had a beautiful home and three amazing, happy children. She beat herself up almost daily for not feeling like her marriage was enough, for wondering what was wrong with her and if she would ever be satisfied. She struggled to reciprocate the love her husband showed her, but the wall around her heart was pretty high.

When we first began working together, Lynne said, "I feel like I don't deserve this. I feel like I don't deserve his love." By the end of our sessions, after she had found her way through a journey of self-forgiveness and become open to the possibility within her marriage, one of the last things she said was, "I deserve this."

And she did. She does. We all do.

Chapter 12:

The Truth about Gratitude

"Gratitude unlocks the fullness of life. It turns what we have into enough, and more."

MELODY BEATTIE

As a life coach, one of the things I commonly hear when speaking to clients who are struggling with their marriage that looks pretty good from the outside but feels empty inside is, "What's wrong with me? I should be grateful."

Then they begin comparing their marriage and their husband to other people who, in their eyes, have it worse than them:

- "At least he doesn't beat me."
- "At least he doesn't lie or cheat."
- "At least he's not like Donna's husband; I couldn't take that."

Comparing our situation to someone else's might make us feel a little better in the moment, but it doesn't change our hearts. It doesn't change how we really feel. It doesn't take away the longing. It just suppresses it for a moment.

If you want to experience a shift in your life, there are precious few things that are more powerful than gratitude. But that shift only occurs when the gratitude is real, when it's sincere.

Using comparison to beat yourself into being grateful is like pouring pink paint over the pain. It appears to provide relief in the moment, but the pain still lingers beneath the surface.

You Can Be Grateful and Still Want Change

There's an assumption that if I'm grateful then I have to accept what-is forever, and so nothing will ever change. There's an illusion of permanence around gratitude, but that isn't real. You can absolutely be truly grateful and still want change. You can genuinely appreciate all that you have and still sit in the expectation for having more. That's a beautiful and powerful place to be.

Want what you want.

If your heart can desire it, then you can have it. Even if you've never seen it before. Even if you've never felt it before. You didn't magically place that desire in your heart, so you can't get rid of it either. You might as well love it a little, comfort it a little, and nurture it a little.

You Can't Curse the Past

You can't curse the past and get the future you want. Your past, your experiences, your relationships, your life lessons brought you to this place. This place where you're desiring more, knowing all that you want to feel and experience, and knowing what you don't want.

I'll give you a personal example.

I am married to an amazing man who is my heart and my home, my passion and my peace. I love Derrick in ways I hadn't even known was possible. And I feel his love for me every day.

This is a second marriage for each of us. His first marriage ended painfully. He used to say to me, "Where were you 20 years ago?" and I answer with all my love and honesty, "We never would have worked 20 years ago." I'm not the same person now as I was then. I had to go through a marriage that showed me what was really important. I had to fall in love deeply with someone and have my heart shattered. I had to make mistakes and learn from them. And by going through all that, I am now able to receive and sustain the kind of adoring love my husband showers upon me.

But I couldn't have that if I had continued to carry anger or bitterness from my first marriage or from the subsequent relationships that hurt me. I have to bless my past experiences because they are what has brought me to here. Even the painful experiences were just contrast helping me to get closer and closer to what I really wanted.

You can't curse your past and create the future you want. So bless it. Appreciate it. Bask in it. Roll around like a puppy in the grass in all that you have and all that you've come to know. From that place, miracles can happen and shifts can occur.

Your Desires Don't End

Oh, and by the way, your desires for more – more love, more light, more ease, more joy – they don't end.

There is no Promised Land where you stop reaching. This does not mean you're greedy. It's not selfish. It's natural to reach for more. It's how we evolve as a universe. It's how we grow individually. It's how we advance our lives and expand our experiences.

You won't ever stop desiring more, but this is not about wanting more material things or wanting your husband to change in more ways. This is a desire for more meaning in your life, more joy filling your days, more people and experiences to appreciate.

We're asking, "Why isn't this marriage enough?"

Your desire for more will never end.

As long as you never stop loving, you'll never stop desiring.

Chapter 13:

The Truth about Your Responsibilities

"Basic human contact – the meeting of eyes, the exchanging of words – is to the psyche what oxygen is to the brain."

MARTHA BECK

The place where we get tripped up on this desire for more is when we're looking outside of ourselves to fulfill that desire. Specifically, we look to our partners to make us feel happy, whole, excited, and fulfilled. But the fulfillment of our desires begins within us and is created through us. Let me explain further.

If you want more passion in your life, are you living passionately? Are you filling your days and prioritizing your life based upon things that you're passionate about? If you're saying that you want more passion in your life, but you're waiting for your husband to make dinner reservations at your favorite restaurant, you're missing the point.

What you want isn't one pleasant night bestowed upon you by someone else (although it's nice when it happens). What you really want is a life filled with passionate experiences, things that make you absolutely light up, and (this is the best part) *you want to create them.*

You're a creator at heart. You wouldn't have it any other way.

If you want more love in your life, are you giving love to others (remember, love isn't only about getting it, it's also about giving it)? Are you being loving toward the people around you? Do you look people in the eyes and really hear what they're saying? Do you smile first? Do you embrace others just because it feels so good?

What you want isn't merely for your husband to say, "I love you," (although it's nice when he does). What you really want is to *feel* love in your life; feel love flowing through you and to you. When you become more loving yourself, you will have an abundance of love in your life. You'll literally become surrounded by it.

You wouldn't have it any other way.

The Power of Presence

One of the most valuable gifts we can give to another human being is our presence. Presence is our undivided attention and genuine interest in another soul, and this is a very loving act.

Lynne and her husband were celebrating their wedding anniversary and she really wanted to try to reconnect with him. They had plans for a dinner out and I asked her what she wanted to feel during the experience. She told me that she wanted to feel at ease, to feel a knowing and a trusting that everything was going to be okay. So we put together a plan. It was a really complex, really difficult, and really intricate plan...

The plan was to *be present*.

That was it.

To really see him.

To really hear him.

To get a sense for what he was most excited about in his life.

To share each other's hearts.

To put the phone down and not let the kids and their logistics, or work, consume the conversation.

To make eye contact.

To slip her hand in his.

To be loving and present.

And to give herself permission to enjoy.

Your Responsibility is Pretty Simple

If you want love, become more loving.

If you want passion, become a more passionate person.

If you want more excitement and adventure, become more exciting and adventurous.

When you do that, you will draw to you the people, places, and experiences that perpetuate that feeling. You won't have to lift a finger, make a decision, or make it happen. *The people who can't be down with that will naturally fade out of the picture.*

Chapter 14:

The Truth about Your Desires

"Passion is energy. Feel the power that comes from focusing on what excites you."

OPRAH WINFREY

My client Elaine had lost touch with what brought her joy. She had three young children and the thought of doing something just because it felt good to her seemed selfish, unattainable, and unnecessary. She didn't have time for joy. She most certainly didn't have time for herself. Since the day she gave birth to her first child, all her wants and desires had moved to the back burner. That was so long ago that she can't even recall what she was ever passionate about.

I'm convinced that there is nothing as simultaneously rewarding and difficult as being a mother. We are taught that to be a *good mother*, we have to put the needs of our children first and always. So we do everything we can – we get them everything they need and want, and we organize our worlds around them. But on the long list of all the things we want to give to our children, how often is *a happy mother* on that list?

Do You Know What Brings You Joy?

If you're like Elaine and you can't even remember what you used to love to do, get curious. Look for clues. What are you doing when you lose track of time? When you think back to the three happiest moments in your life, what were you doing?

If you know what brings you joy but you don't have time in your life to pursue those interests and passions, then it's time to get intentional. It doesn't require you to completely drop the ball on your life. I know you're busy, and some days you may feel like you're being buried alive. But ten minutes is what I'm asking you to gift to yourself. Ten minutes each day to do something just because it feels good to do it.

Don't overthink this. Sometimes my feeling good time is spent treating myself to a latte. Sometimes it's walking outside and taking a few deep breaths. Sometimes it's taking a bath, reading a book, or watching a movie. I love to travel, so sometimes it's planning a trip. I love to cook and bake, take walks, play catch with my dogs and watch them run.

What do you love to do?

Fit it into your day. Just make it happen. Prove to yourself that you're important.

Doing so doesn't make anyone else in your life any less important, it just puts you and your heart on the list of those who need you.

When our cars run out of gas, we don't pull into the gas station, lay our heads on the wheel, and cry out, "Oh I give up." No. We make the small effort to get out of our cars and fill up our tanks. That's what I'm asking you to do.

We also don't say, "I guess I'll just sit here at this gas station forever until somebody notices that my tank is empty and is kind enough to fill it up for me." You could be waiting a long time.

We're Supposed to Feel Good

I know we've been taught from a young age that we need to go to school and get good grades so that we can get a good job and make something of ourselves. Then we should fall in love, get married, and have kids. We will work really hard for a long time, pay bills, get sick, and then die. And sprinkled in there are moments of goodness, moments of joy.

But it doesn't have to be that way. We've made it seem like it should be that way. And if we made it that way, if we did this, made these assumptions about life, then we can change it.

Nearly every day, I wake up and set the intention that I want to feel as good as I can feel. Even when it's hard, even when it's far from fun, I care about how I feel and I want to feel as good as I can, as often as I can. Just because I'm a life coach doesn't mean I don't have bad days or that I somehow lead a charmed life. I do have the tools to move me through those bad times quickly and most importantly, I use them.

Take a lesson from babies and puppies. You will rarely ask a child if he wants to go to the park to play and hear him say, "Well, I don't think I've done enough today to earn that. Maybe tomorrow."

No! Instead what you'll hear is, "Yes! Yes! Yes! And then can we go for ice cream? And then can we go to the toy store?" More fun. More light. More joy.

I have two small puppies and they're such beautiful teachers for me. They love to go out for walks. Then, they want to play ball in the house or roughhouse together. They want to be petted and loved on. They take naps. Oh, and then they want treats. It's like they're constantly saying, "What now? What now? What now?" More fun. More light. More joy.

Life is supposed to feel good. It's supposed to be joyful. Wanting to feel good is not being indulgent. It's our birthright. We just forgot that along the way.

There's Nothing Like a Loss to Give Us Perspective

After a battle with colon cancer that she ultimately lost, my client Camille's mother passed away. Camille was incredibly close to her mother. With her last breaths, her mother gave Camille some wisdom that has stuck with her. Her mother told her to "Just be happy." Camille thinks about that a lot now, and it's made her realize how short and how precious life really is.

It's too short to worry about the past or attempt to control the future.

It's too short to not tell the truth – to yourself and everyone else.

It's too short for false friendships and people who want to keep you small.

It's too short to not tell the people you love how you feel.

It's too short to not squeeze in as much joy and love as possible. More fun. More light. More joy.

Chapter 15:

The Truth about Why This Is Hard

"Obstacles are put in our way to see if what we want is worth fighting for."

UNKNOWN

There is nothing more important in our lives than our relationships, particularly our closest relationships. At times, relationships can feel like the hardest part of our lives. Maybe that's because they're so important, or maybe it's because our relationships involve other people so it feels out of our control.

If you're asking the question, "Why isn't this marriage enough?" then you know how hard it feels to stay in the relationship and you know how hard it would be to leave the relationship.

If you stay, there's the fear that you'll be unhappy and discontented forever.

If you leave, there's the fear that you will be judged by everyone around you for leaving such a *good guy*. Plus, what if everyone is right and the grass isn't actually greener on the other side? What if you hurt your husband and your kids and it was all for nothing and you aren't even really happier?

But remember that you don't have to choose between giving up all your longings and desires or giving up your husband. You get to want both. You get to want to have a great partner by your side *and* a life filled with love, happiness, passion, and light. It will require that you change the rules a bit for yourself:

- You'll take responsibility for your own happiness.
- You'll get intentional about pursuing your dreams and desires.
- You'll stop trying to change him so you can feel better.
- You'll become the person who loves (rather than just looking for love to be focused at you).

- You'll teach him a new way to treat you; one that aligns more with who you really are and what you really want to create in your life.
- You'll express your needs and make space for yourself and your heart in your life.
- You'll do whatever you need to do to feel good and invite in more fun, more light, and more joy.

Now, it's easy to say those things, but let's take "You'll take responsibility for your own happiness" as an example. How do you do that when your husband comes home with some horrible news? For instance, my client Camille was ready to leave her husband and he came home and told her after his visit to the dermatologist that they thought he might have skin cancer.

It's one thing to hear the concept of *teaching him a new way to treat you,* but the truth is that it took you a long time to teach him how to treat you the old way, the way that doesn't feel so good. How will you consistently act so that he will treat you differently? That can feel like trying to turn an aircraft carrier.

Colleen wanted her husband to treat her respectfully, listen to her opinion, and not dismiss her children from her first marriage. But she had allowed his disrespect, not listening to her opinions, and disrespect for her kids for so long that each time she tried to stand up for herself it turned into a fight and she just wanted to give up.

And then there's the concept of *becoming the loving person,* even when you don't feel love coming back from him in return. That's a great goal, but one that many people abandon because it's uncomfortable. It's hard to be loving toward someone who's hard to love, at times.

It's All Hard

What you're learning about in this book is a new way of being. We go in looking for what's wrong with us, for why we can't just love this good guy. We struggle with how to live in a disconnected marriage or with the decision of whether to leave our marriage and blow up our lives because we can't see another way. Living from this place is hard. Living in a mediocre marriage is also hard. It's all hard. Relationships are hard. But it's so worth it.

What you've learned so far is that you actually have a lot more influence over the happiness in your life than maybe you originally thought. And once you start to put some of these simple but profound practices into place in your daily life, you will stop looking for your husband to do something different, or to be someone different, and you won't feel so powerless and stuck.

Also, as you begin to make changes for yourself, you'll be gathering information. As you change, it will cause others around you to react – either in good ways or bad ways. Their reactions to you becoming happier will contain valuable information. If they're happy for you and want to be along for the ride, wonderful. If they're curious about how they could do the same thing for themselves, share what you've learned. And if they're threatened by your newfound happiness, then they don't really have your best interests at heart, and that's good information to know.

Want more Soulful Truth Telling?

- - - - - - - - - - - - - - - - - - -

Get any of my free ebooks
on love and relationships:
SharonPopeGoodness.com

Section Four:

Your Relationship 2.0

Chapter 16:

The Truth about Conscious Re-Connecting

"You never lose by loving. You always lose by holding back."

BARBARA DE ANGELIS

You may have heard of *conscious uncoupling*. Gwyneth Paltrow and Chris Martin made that a talked about process for intentionally getting through a divorce peacefully. You can also apply that same philosophy to re-connecting with your husband, if that's your desire.

Here's what it will take:

- You're going to have to let him in. You're going to have to stop holding back and keeping him at arm's distance.
- You're going to have to share your most heartfelt feelings and your deepest fears about the state of your relationship. You can't limit your conversations to only kids and logistics.
- You're going to have to know what you want and express those needs... again and again and again.
- You're going to have to meet him where he is and speak to him in a manner that he can understand. (Hint: That might be a different way than you've done in the past.)
- You're going to have to seek out ways to make him feel loved and you're going to have to be able to receive the way he shows his love to you.
- Your heart needs to be fully present. You can't have your heart wrapped up in someone else or even mildly entertaining the thought of being with another.
- And if you stay together and you want to stay connected to him, you'll have to keep doing all of those things.

If you do those things and the marriage still ends, it's okay. You can look at that truth in the mirror each day, because you will know that you did all you could.

Alternatively, however, doing those things could open the door to the genuine possibility of re-connecting with the man you once loved (and maybe still love).

Soften Up

I was on a trip with my best friend when we met a lovely mother and daughter who were from Louisiana and traveling together. Their husband and father, respectively, had passed away three years prior. I asked the daughter what she remembered most about her father from when she was growing up, and she told me that he used to always tell her, "Soften up, Baby."

What he meant by that was that she was too hard on people; she expected too much of others and of herself; she pushed too hard and forced too much. So my friend and I proceeded to spend the rest of the weekend telling each other to "Soften up, Baby," in our best Cajun accents. It was a good reminder. We don't have to try so hard. We don't have to push or to force things to happen. We can allow ourselves some softness in our lives and in our relationships.

The next day, I hopped on the phone with my client Lynne for our coaching call and she said, with no prompting at all from me, "I feel like I've hardened myself to the one person I need to be soft with."

There was something divine about that exchange and about the timing of that message from a father who clearly had plenty of wisdom to impart, which I was then able to share with my client: "Soften up, Baby."

Do We Want This or Do We Only *Want* to Want This?

Marilyn knew her husband was a good man and a great father. But, over the years, she had lost her attraction to him. Although they rarely fought, she never wanted to have sex and she wasn't drawn to him anymore. If there was a switch that she could have flipped to make herself attracted to her husband again, she would have flipped that switch in a heartbeat.

In addition to needing a magic pill, we also now need a magic switch. That would make this so much easier. Unfortunately, that doesn't exist either.

So, although Marilyn thought she wanted her marriage to work, she actually didn't. She wanted to *want* it to work. She wanted to want that man and that marriage, but the truth was that she didn't want him or the marriage anymore.

She didn't want to create a problem if there wasn't one. She didn't want to hurt her husband. She didn't want to disrupt her kids' lives, even though the youngest was going to be a junior in high school and the others were already in college and on their own. She didn't want to have to sell the house and move. She didn't want to be judged or thought of as a crazy person, since you can't exactly go around telling everyone that you're no longer attracted to your husband and didn't ever want to have sex with him. That's a private, personal matter that she didn't even want to tell *him*, much less their family, friends and the kids.

Sometimes we genuinely want the marriage to work. We want to re-connect or to create a new connection. But sometimes we just want to want that. There's a distinction, and it's an important one. It's important to know where you are so that you can be honest with yourself about what you want.

Chapter 17:

The Truth about the Future of Your Marriage

"…not every relationship can be healed. In fact, sometimes the most healing act is to leave a relationship."

GABRIELE VUCCI

I f you've followed me for any period of time, you know I'm not the coach who's going to tell you, "Suck it up. Give up on those dreams and desires. You'll never have what you want, and it would be really hard at your age to find love again, so maybe staying in an unhappy marriage is better than being alone."

Nope. Wrong coach.

If your marriage can be saved, it will need to include all of your dreams and desires. And his, too.

It will need to re-emerge as a different version of your relationship. Think of it as the 2.0 version of you as a couple.

It will have to look and feel different than how it looked before.

How you interact and connect with each other will need to evolve.

The parts that no longer serve the marriage will need to be pruned away.

And the parts that work well will need to be brought into the light and nurtured.

There's No Going Backward

My client Krissy had a perfectly fine marriage. There wasn't anything horribly wrong. There wasn't great conflict, but there wasn't great connection either. Until, that is, that she found a deep, meaningful connection in an emotional affair with someone she worked with. She shared her struggles with him. She shared her joys with him. She felt seen and heard and understood. She said it was as though he could see right into her heart.

Now the marriage was broken. Now it was in trouble.

Even though the relationship with the other man ended abruptly once her husband found out, Krissy knew something she hadn't known previously. She knew what it felt like to have a deep connection with another soul.

I've heard that described in a lot of ways that are similar versions of the same things:

- It's like going from seeing everything in black and white to seeing everything in full color. You didn't know about that kind of beauty.
- It's like eating only apples your whole life and discovering what steak, figs, fresh herbs, and strawberries taste like. You didn't know something could taste so good.
- It felt like you had been sleepwalking through your life and now you feel alive again. You didn't know there was any other way to feel.

Once you know that feeling, there is no going back.

I'm not saying, "There is no going back to your husband." I'm saying, "There is no way to pretend you don't know what figs taste like and go back to only eating apples." You now know something at a very deep level that you can't simply erase from your mind or pretend you don't know. So, it's not possible to go back to your marriage exactly the way it was. You can't go back to seeing in black and white, only eating apples, and sleepwalking through your life.

You have to create something new together. And it needs to involve not only full-color images and feeling alive again, but also apples, steak, figs, fresh herbs, and strawberries. It needs to include all of it.

Since Krissy had never had that with her husband, she hadn't known it was possible.

You Can't Get It Wrong

What if you can't get it *wrong*? What if you knew you couldn't make the *wrong* decision?

I'm a big fan of the warmer/colder game. Remember that game you played when you were a child where you would hide an object and then direct the other person about where to find it by saying, "Warmer, warmer, warmer," as they were getting closer to it and, "Colder, colder, colder," as they were moving further away from it?

That's how we can live our lives.

You take a step and you see how it feels – warmer or colder?

You take another step you see how it feels. If it's warmer keep stepping in that direction. If it feels colder, stop and pay attention. Something's not right. Back up and take a different step.

Many of us have never been taught to pay attention to how we feel. Nor have we been taught that we're supposed to feel good (warmer).

Using this as a tool in your marriage, you can guide yourself closer and closer to the happy, connected life you envision for yourself.

Try sharing your heart with your husband. Have a conversation that doesn't involve work or kids. How did it feel? Warmer? Colder? Awkward is okay, especially at first.

But did it feel good? If yes, then great, that's warmer, so remove one block from that wall you've built around your heart and be prepared to take another step.

Did he criticize you or make you feel small? If so, then that's colder. Pay attention. Take a step in another direction.

If you keep taking steps and gathering information, you'll find yourself – sooner rather than later – on the path your soul came here to enjoy.

Not Every Relationship Should Last Forever

As a truth-telling life coach, I abandoned my judgments of right and wrong, good and bad a long time ago. They didn't serve me and they most certainly didn't serve my clients (although I'm sure it frustrates my devout Catholic father to no end).

There are a lot of people who will tell you that leaving your marriage is *wrong* and that you're a *bad* person if you do that. But who am I – or for that matter, who is anyone – to judge your journey? They're not living in your heart or in your life or walking in your shoes.

As you know by now, I believe that every important relationship we have is a teacher for us. I believe they each have lessons that we could only have learned through them or gifts that we could only have received through them. I always believe there's something that can be learned, some meaning that can be found, from each of our most important relationships.

But I don't automatically say that every relationship should last forever and if it doesn't it was *wrong*.

My marriage to my first husband wasn't *wrong*; it was a piece to the puzzle that brought me to here, to helping other women navigate through their own relationship challenges. It was a big piece of my journey that made me a better wife to Derrick today.

My client Marilyn's marriage – even though it ended – wasn't *wrong*; it produced three beautiful children.

I can even argue that the emotional affair Krissy had wasn't *wrong*, because it woke her up from simply going through the motions of her life and it showed her what a deep, intimate connection felt like. If she can feel it with one person, she can feel it with another person.

Every experience is there for you.

Every relationship is there for you.

In every moment you get another opportunity to take another step.

And you can't get it wrong.

Chapter 18:

The Truth about Your Focus

"We cannot focus upon the weaknesses of one another and evoke strengths. You cannot focus upon the things you think they are doing wrong, and evoke the things that will make you feel better."

ABRAHAM-HICKS

You may have heard the saying, *what you focus on expands.* It's true. But that rule doesn't make any distinction between positive things and negative things. Our focus expands whatever is being focused upon.

Have you ever known someone who was always negative, always looking for what could go wrong and preparing for the worst? Did that person live a life of ease and joy? No, because that would be impossible.

Have you ever known someone who was wonderfully nice to be around, who was always really positive, and you felt better when you were with them? Did they have a life of pain and despair? No, because that can't happen.

You can't create a happy life when the only raw materials are only sadness and despair, regret and anger.

So it's important to place your attention on the things you want more of in your life:

- More laughter with your kids and grandkids.
- More long talks with your best friend.
- More people and experiences to love.

That's how you can create more laughter, more connection, and more love in your life. You will draw more of those experiences toward you as you take the time to focus on them and appreciate them when they show up.

The Same Is True in Our Relationships

Your husband has lots of pieces that make up the whole of who he is. Like you, he has a primary self and a shadow self. For each of those traits, we could sit here and judge them as good traits or bad traits (that is, unless you went ahead and dropped all the judgments, along with me, as we discussed in the last chapter).

As you think about your husband, what are the things you really like about him? Maybe he's fun to be with. Maybe he's funny and makes you laugh. Maybe he is organized, creative, or hard-working.

Take a moment and think about a few traits that you really appreciate about him.

Now, if you make the conscious effort to focus on those attributes, the ones you really enjoy in him, you will literally draw more of that out in him. By really noticing the times when he makes you laugh, by thinking about those moments in the car while you're driving, by thinking about them while you're in a boring meeting at work, or by telling your friends about the experience, you will get more of that from him. He won't know why, but you will.

As you look for more reasons to appreciate those qualities of his that you like, their prominence and importance will take up more space in your awareness of him.

But here's the thing: You can't focus upon those great qualities so that you can change him (were not going backward here, only forward). Focus on the qualities that you really love and admire about him *because* it feels good to do so. Intentionally focus on your favorite aspects of him because it feels a lot better than focusing on all the ways he falls short in your eyes. *That* will never feel good. And, if you recall, feeling good is the whole point.

Don't Fill up on Lima Beans

When we go to a buffet that has 100 different items all laid out beautifully for us, we take great care to select the items we like the most. We fill up on the things that make us feel good and that we really enjoy eating.

It's a shame we don't take as much care in making decisions about the things we focus on in other people – especially our husbands.

I am not a fan of lima beans. So I would never go to a buffet and head straight for the lima beans and fill my plate with them so that nothing else could fit. I would never do that and I doubt you would either.

If you were lactose intolerant, you would never head to that same buffet and load your plate up with cottage cheese. You wouldn't do it because it wouldn't make you feel good.

If we can take that much care selecting what we want to put into our bodies, maybe we can take a little bit more care with choosing thoughts that feel good to think about regarding our husbands. Maybe we can focus a little more on the things we really enjoy about him and just turn our heads away a bit when it comes to the things we enjoy less or the pieces that seem to be missing.

Whenever I find myself picking at my husband about what he should be doing that he isn't, or what he is doing but shouldn't, I will stop and say to myself, "Oh, there I go again, picking lima beans." He doesn't know I say that, but I guarantee you he can feel the impact of it.

Chapter 19:

The Truth about Therapy Compared to Coaching

"The details of what you're fighting over are negligible compared to your innermost experience begging to be heard."
SEVIN PHILIPS

Many of my clients who are struggling in their marriages attend marriage counseling with their husbands, sometimes in addition to working with me, sometimes prior to their individual work with me.

These clients will share with me the context of their conversations and progress (or lack thereof) as a result of those therapy sessions.

One of the problems I see repeatedly in their conversations is that they're not getting to the heart of the matter.

My client Abbey goes to marriage counseling with her husband twice a week, where they discuss what's *not* working in the relationship – mostly from Abbey's perspective, since she's the one who's unhappy in the relationship.

When she says she doesn't feel at home in her own home, the counselor and her husband suggest she go buy some things she likes to put in their home, to make it represent her style and tastes more. But that's not the real problem.

When she shares that she doesn't feel heard, the counselor teaches her husband better listening skills. But his ability to listen isn't the issue.

When Abbey laments that she and her husband hardly spend any time together, the therapist suggests a weekly date night. But the time itself isn't the real issue.

Abbey is supposed to supply the reasons for why she's unhappy and unfulfilled in her marriage, and then the marriage counselor provides suggestions for each of those reasons, so that Abbey's husband can react, resolve, or fix it. Reason by reason they do this – every week.

But in all that time of identifying and attempting to slap a bandage on each individual problem, they're avoiding the root cause of the problem. They're not talking about the heart of the matter. They're not discussing that in Abbey's marriage she feels invisible, empty, unheard, unseen, unimportant, and disconnected. They're also not discussing what Abbey *wants* to feel in her life and marriage.

It's time to take the conversation much deeper.

What Abbey wants is to feel adventurous in her life and full of possibilities.

She wants a marriage that isn't only *fine*. She wants a marriage that's *extraordinary*.

She even wants to have a few butterflies when her husband looks at her and smiles.

When she lays her head down on her pillow at night next to her beloved, Abbey wants to feel warm, secure, and peaceful. She wants to feel that there's no place else she'd rather be.

If you're going to go get help for your marriage and get something really meaningful from it, it's important to get at the heart of the matter: What's the root of your hurt, and have you expressed that hurt to your husband?

Does he think you're nagging about helping with the kids and spending more time with the family? Or does he realize that you feel like you have a warm body next to you, but are still alone and abandoned in your own life?

Does he think you're overreacting again? Or does he know that when he spends too much money without consulting you it makes you feel unsafe and distrustful?

We need to stop talking about the day-to-day irritants and begin discussing how those instances make you *feel*. We need to discuss the hurt. We need a deeper level of conversation to occur in order to make meaningful progress.

Therapy Isn't Bad – It's Just Different than Coaching

I could bash marriage counseling or therapy, but that would be disingenuous. I'm a product of therapy myself. After my divorce, I saw a great therapist and, once a week, he provided me a beautiful space in which to melt down and begin to understand myself better.

My therapist helped me understand how I had gotten to where I was, but he couldn't pick me up, brush me off, and move me forward. Obviously, that's not true about every therapist. Just as with life coaches, there are good ones and others who aren't as good.

I've found that, in therapy, you can spend more time than is necessary looking back to understand why you are where you are. Although that's really important if they're going to diagnose you, it doesn't automatically help with going forward, especially if the root of the issue isn't discovered or clarified.

Coaching tends to be more forward-focused. Where is it you're trying to get to, and what's keeping you from getting there? If the obstacle to getting to where you want to go is something in your past that we need to clean up – like a thought, a belief, a fear that's keeping you stuck – then let's go there, by all means! But because I'm not going to diagnose you, I'm sort of like the GPS in your car: We find out where you want to go and I guide you there. If you want to be in the driver's seat of your life, I can be your driver's ed instructor.

Your Girlfriends as Support

When I was struggling in my first marriage, I wasn't yet a Master Life Coach. I didn't even know what a life coach was. I struggled to just appreciate what I had, and forget about connecting with my husband. I tried to get him to change. I badgered myself into believing that there was clearly something wrong with me, since I was the one who was so unhappy. That process was much longer and more difficult than it needed to be.

As is the case for most women, my best girlfriends were my first line of support. They would let me cry on their shoulders and they encouraged me along the way. They would tell me, "It will be okay," and, "You deserve to be happy."

The problem with telling and retelling the story of how our husbands aren't the men we need them to be is that it keeps us stuck in that story. Our girlfriends who love us will listen to that story for as long as we need to tell it, because they want to be there for us. That's what best girlfriends do: They love us through the pain and provide a softer landing for us when we fall down.

Many women contact me when they realize that the support of friends isn't enough, or they fear that their friends are getting sick of hearing the same story over and over.

Your friends are going to love you. That's their job. But they're not going to challenge you. They're also not able to pick you up, brush you off and help you move forward in a meaningful way.

Your Lighthouse

People ask me all the time how it is that I do the work I do. They wonder how I can listen to stories all day about marriages that are in trouble and falling apart, and then not go home depressed.

Here's how I think about it:

When you're sailing on the ocean in the dark, I can't help you if I hop into another boat and try to find you and guide you somehow. If I'm in the dark with you, I can't help you.

However, I can be the lighthouse. I can keep calling you toward me over and over again, holding a steady glow so you can find your way through the darkness, and lighting the way for your safe return home.

That's how I do the beautiful work I consider myself privileged to do.

Chapter 20:

My Wish for You

"And the day came when the risk to remain tight in a bud was more painful than the risk it took to blossom."

ANAÏS NIN

You came to this book asking an important question: "Why isn't this marriage enough?" It probably haunted you for months, or even years, before you found this resource. I'm glad you found it.

I have no agenda for your life.

You may use the principles outlined in this book and your marriage may become not only *enough*, but even more than you could have hoped for. That is possible.

You may apply these principles in your life and in your marriage and your marriage may still end. But you'll know that you tried, and there's a certain amount of peace that comes with the simple knowledge and awareness of having done the best you could.

My wish for you is…

- That you have opened your heart to the possibilities that exist for you, for your life, and for your marriage.
- That you make yourself a priority in your own life.
- That you take better care of your heart and your marriage.
- That you set the intention to do whatever it takes to feel good and live happily.
- That you know you deserve the kind of relationship you desire.
- That you know that – no matter what happens in your marriage – you can be happy.
- That you know that you're not alone.
- That you know that there's nothing wrong with you; that you don't need to be *fixed*.

It's So Worth It

Falling in love is so easy it feels effortless.

Trying to sustain a love takes quite a bit of effort, along with a healthy dose of self-awareness and patience, forgiveness and acceptance.

Falling back in love when love has been lost is more difficult.

And trying to save a marriage that's on life support will require everything you've got to give. I'm glad that you now have more tools in your toolbox to work with.

This work, this journey that you've embarked upon, isn't easy. If it was easy everyone would do it and we would all be walking around blissfully happy and in loving and connected marriages. But those who embrace the journey and look at the whole of life as an experience leading toward more meaning and more growth, more love and more joy, are in for one heck of a ride! And when you're enjoying the ride – the ride that is your life – it's all so worth it.

Your Guide

Some people can pick up a book, read it, and completely integrate it into their lives. Most of us, however, cannot.

I don't know about you, but I've read books on weight loss and, at the end of the book, I knew a little bit more, but I hadn't lost 40 pounds.

Most of us need support and accountability in order to really integrate new tools and insights into our lives.

If you find that you'd like a guide for this journey, I hope you'll keep me in mind (www.sharonpopetruth.com/truth-clarity-session).

Acknowledgements

T hank you to the hundreds of women who have placed their trust in me. I will continue to be the lighthouse for you when you cannot see what's ahead, calling you forward so you can step into and bask in your own light.

Thank you to Angela Lauria, who held the space for me to become the woman I need to become to do this work in this world in a big, big way.

Appreciation for my publisher, Morgan James for pouring their gifts into this book so that it can reach the women who need it.

Thank you to my soul sister, Traci Snyder. Some of the greatest gifts I've received in this life came from and through you. I love you with my whole heart.

This book holds a special place in my heart. It was written in Tuscany – probably my favorite place in the world, the place where I found so much healing after the divorce from my first husband and where I found healing after some other painful heartbreak. Plus, this book was written alongside some incredible women who were creating their own books. Cassie and Jill, you are a consistent source of inspiration to me.

This book was written as a love letter to honor the journey of some incredibly brave women: my clients, who, by allowing me to share their stories, might make another woman somewhere who's struggling know that she's not alone and that there is a path through the darkest and deepest questions in our lives.

Most importantly, through this book I've sought to bring love back into a marriage when it's been lost. Sometimes that love leads to staying and re-connecting with your partner; sometimes it doesn't. But that love always, *always* leads you back home to your heart.

About the Author

Sharon Pope is a certified Martha Beck Master Life Coach and a five-time international best-selling author. She helps women get the clarity they need and heal from their most painful, intimate relationships.

Sharon is author of a series of five books all dedicated to love and relationships. The series includes:

- ***Why is Love so Hard to Find?*** – for women who want a soulful, deep, and lasting love in their lives.
- ***Am I in the Wrong Marriage?*** – for women who are trying to determine if they should stay and recommit to their marriage or lovingly release it.

- *Why Can't I Get Over Him?* – for women struggling with moving on after a painful breakup or divorce.
- *I Know It's Over. Now What?* – for women who know their marriage is over, but don't know what to do next.
- *Why Isn't This Marriage Enough?* – for women whose marriage and life from the outside looks picture-perfect, but inside feels empty and alone.

Sharon is also the author of the memoir, *Life, Love, Lies & Lessons: A Journey through Truth to Find an Authentic Life*. Her writing has been published dozens of times in various online venues.

She received her undergraduate education from Ohio University, and an MBA from Ashland University. Prior to coaching, Sharon was in corporate marketing for nearly twenty years.

Sharon lives in Columbus, Ohio, with the love of her life, husband, and spiritual partner, Derrick.

Tell the Truth. Show up in Love. Live in Freedom.

Facebook – www.facebook.com/SharonPopeTruthCoach

Pinterest – www.pinterest.com/sharonpopetruth

Twitter – @SharonPopeTruth

Thank You

Morgan James
Speakers Group

↗ www.TheMorganJamesSpeakersGroup.com

We connect Morgan James published
authors with live and online events
and audiences whom will benefit
from their expertise.

Morgan James makes all of our titles available
through the Library for All Charity Organization.

www.LibraryForAll.org